BRACKETIVITY
SCARES

You Decide the Winner!

By Vero Velázquez

Andrews McMeel
PUBLISHING®

Andrews McMeel Publishing
a division of Andrews McMeel Universal
1130 Walnut Street, Kansas City, Missouri 64106

www.andrewsmcmeel.com

24 25 26 27 28 RLP 10 9 8 7 6 5 4 3 2 1

ISBN: 978-1-5248-9229-6

Editor: Cindy Harris
Art Director: Tiffany Meairs
Production Editor: Brianna Westervelt
Production Manager: Tamara Haus

Made by:
Shenzhen Reliance Printing Co., Ltd.
Address and place of manufacturer:
25 Longshan Industrial Zone, Nanling,
Longgang District, Shenzhen, China, 518114
1st Printing - 3/11/2024

ATTENTION: SCHOOLS AND BUSINESSES
Andrews McMeel books are available at quantity discounts with bulk purchase for educational, business, or sales promotional use. For information, please e-mail the Andrews McMeel Publishing Special Sales Department:
sales@amuniversal.com.

SCARES

Boo! It's never too early (or too late) to get into the spooky spirit. What's the scariest monster? The best horror movie? The tastiest Halloween candy? How should you decorate your pumpkin?

In your hands (or claws) is a very special, spooky-themed Bracketivity book. Within these pages, you'll be able to pick your favorite "thing" in each category. But it's not just a "pick and go" situation—you'll have to fill each bracket to determine your winner!

Think about each answer carefully because it determines your next round of brackets. Or go with your gut feeling—really, there are no wrong answers! And at the end of the book, you'll even get to make your own Bracketivities to share with family and friends.

So get your wands, claws, talons, and hands ready—it's time to get going! You decide who wins.

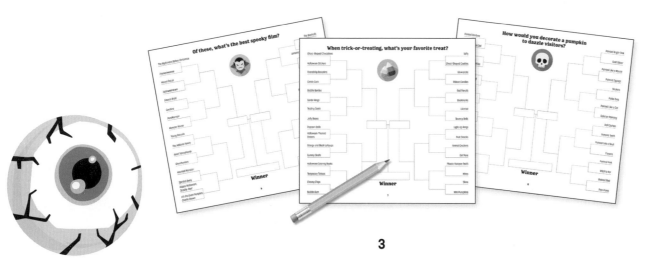

What's the best thing to do on Halloween?

BRACKETIVITY EXAMPLE

Here's an example **Bracketivity** that's filled out. It's what your author would pick. Don't worry—if you disagree, you'll get to fill out your own **Bracketivity** on the next page.

Carve Pumpkins

Bob for Apples — Carve Pumpkins

Trick-or-Treat — Trick-or-Treat

Visit a Haunted House

Trick-or-Treat

Go on a Hayride — Go on a Hayride

Venture into a Corn Maze

Visit a Pumpkin Patch

Visit a Pumpkin Patch — Visit a Pumpkin Patch

Pick Apples

Trick-or-Treat

Put Up Decorations

Watch a Halloween Movie — Watch a Halloween Movie

Read Tarot Cards — Read Spooky Stories

Read Spooky Stories — Read Spooky Stories

Read Spooky Stories

Make Popcorn Balls — Make Popcorn Balls

Host a Costume Party

Make a Costume from Scratch — Make a Costume from Scratch — Make Popcorn Balls

Sing a Halloween Song

Write a Ghost Story — Write a Ghost Story

Attend a Parade

Go on a Ghost Tour

Go on a Ghost Tour — Go on a Ghost Tour

Break Open a Piñata

Go on a Ghost Tour

Eat Candy

Watch a Scary Show — Watch a Scary Show

Watch a Scary Show

Watch a Scary Show

Drink Apple Cider

Play a Spooky Game — Play a Spooky Game

Play a Spooky Game

Go on a Ghost Tour

Fill Out Bracketivity Scares

Volunteer at a Community Event

Volunteer at a Community Event — Volunteer at a Community Event

Bake Halloween Cookies

Play a Halloween Board Game

Shop for a Costume

Play a Halloween Board Game — Play a Halloween Board Game

Play a Halloween Board Game

Fill Out Bracketivity Scares

Make Toilet Paper Mummies

Make Slime — Make Slime

Make Slime

Fill Out Bracketivity Scares

Fill Out *Bracketivity Scares* — Fill Out *Bracketivity Scares*

Decorate Halloween Masks

Trick-or-Treat

Go on a Ghost Tour

Go on a Ghost Tour
Winner

What's the best thing to do on Halloween?

Carve Pumpkins

Bob for Apples

Trick-or-Treat

Visit a Haunted House

Go on a Hayride

Venture into a Corn Maze

Visit a Pumpkin Patch

Pick Apples

Put Up Decorations

Watch a Halloween Movie

Read Tarot Cards

Read Spooky Stories

Make Popcorn Balls

Host a Costume Party

Make a Costume from Scratch

Sing a Halloween Song

Write a Ghost Story

Attend a Parade

Go on a Ghost Tour

Break Open a Piñata

Eat Candy

Watch a Scary Show

Drink Apple Cider

Play a Spooky Game

Volunteer at a Community Event

Bake Halloween Cookies

Shop for a Costume

Play a Halloween Board Game

Make Toilet Paper Mummies

Make Slime

Fill Out *Bracketivity Scares*

Decorate Halloween Masks

Winner

Of these, what's the best spooky film?

The Nightmare Before Christmas

Frankenweenie

Hocus Pocus

Halloweentown

Corpse Bride

Coraline

ParaNorman

Monster House

The Little Vampire

The Addams Family

Hotel Transylvania

Ghostbusters

Haunted Mansion

Spirited Away

Happy Halloween, Scooby-Doo!

It's the Great Pumpkin, Charlie Brown

Winner

The Boxtrolls

Young Frankenstein

Lemony Snicket's A Series of Unfortunate Events

Hocus Pocus 2

Casper

Jaws

Wallace & Gromit: The Curse of the Were-Rabbit

Maleficent

Goosebumps

A Babysitter's Guide to Monster Hunting

The House with a Clock in Its Walls

Beetlejuice

E.T. the Extra-Terrestrial

The Witches

Labyrinth

Monsters, Inc.

When trick-or-treating, what's your favorite treat?

Ghost-Shaped Chocolates

Halloween Stickers

Friendship Bracelets

Candy Corn

Bubble Bottles

Spider Rings

Trading Cards

Jelly Beans

Popcorn Balls

Halloween-Themed Erasers

Orange and Black Lollipops

Gummy Skulls

Halloween Coloring Books

Temporary Tattoos

Cheesy Chips

Bubble Gum

Taffy

Ghost-Shaped Cookies

Glow Sticks

Ribbon Candies

Red Pencils

Bookmarks

Licorice

Bouncy Balls

Light-Up Rings

Fruit Snacks

Animal Crackers

Gel Pens

Plastic Vampire Teeth

Mints

Slime

Mini Pumpkins

Winner

How would you decorate a pumpkin to dazzle visitors?

Painted Rainbow

Painted Like an Owl

Sequins

Painted Ghost-White

Washi Tape

Painted Black and Yellow Stripes

Painted Black

Painted Purple

Painted Silver

Fairy Crown

Googly Eyes

Painted with a Black Cat

Painted Teal

Brown and Red Leaves

Push-in Faces

Wrapped in Toilet Paper

Painted Bright Pink

Gold Glitter

Painted Like a Mouse

Painted Zigzags

Stickers

Polka Dots

Painted Like a Cat

Splatter Painting

Doll Clothes

Vampire Teeth

Painted Like a Skull

Flowers

Painted Pink

Witch's Hat

Painted Red

Pom-Poms

Winner

Who's the scariest?

Vampire

Zombie

Ghost

Giant Spider

Your Best Friend
When They're Mad

Frankenstein's
Monster

Ghoul

Baba Yaga

Yeti

Skeleton

Medusa

Your Teacher

Swamp Monster

Robot

Mouse

Witch

Werewolf

Poltergeist

Banshee

Chupacabra

Cyclops

Clown

Your Coach

Sea Monster

Troll

Butterfly

Grizzly Bear

The Headless
Horseman

Ogre

Boogeyman

Mummy

Your Parents When You
Forget to Do the Dishes

Winner

Of these, which haunted place would you most want to visit (if you could guarantee returning home safely)? Hint: If you haven't heard of one of these haunted places before, look it up!

The French Quarter (New Orleans, Louisiana)

The Bermuda Triangle (North Atlantic Ocean)

The Forbidden City (Beijing, China)

The Kehoe House (Savannah, Georgia)

Raynham Hall (Norfolk, England)

Area 51 (Nevada)

La Isla de las Muñecas (Mexico City, Mexico)

The Alamo (San Antonio, Texas)

Bhangarh Fort (Rajasthan, India)

The Lizzie Borden House (Fall River, Massachusetts)

Château de Brissac (Maine-et-Loire, France)

Stonehenge (Salisbury, England)

The Catacombs (Paris, France)

The Witch House (Salem, Massachusetts)

Casa Loma (Toronto, Canada)

Tomb of Tutankhamun (Valley of the Kings, Egypt)

Bran Castle (Bran, Romania)

The Wreck of the Titanic (North Atlantic Ocean)

Grand Central Station (New York, New York)

Castle of Good Hope (Cape Town, South Africa)

The Haunted Mansion (Disneyland, Anaheim, California)

Taj Mahal (Agra, India)

St. Augustine Lighthouse (St. Augustine, Florida)

Port Arthur (Tasmania, Australia)

Monte Cristo Homestead (New South Wales, Australia)

Edinburgh Castle (Edinburgh, Scotland)

La Recoleta Cemetery (Buenos Aires, Argentina)

The RMS Queen Mary (Long Beach, California)

Himeji Castle (Himeji, Japan)

Tower of London (London, England)

Tao Dan Park (Ho Chi Minh City, Vietnam)

The Winchester Mystery House (San Jose, California)

Winner

You're decorating for a Halloween party! Which decoration is a must-have?

Cotton Cobwebs

Jack-o'-Lanterns

Plastic Spiders

Styrofoam Headstones

Tissue Paper Ghosts

Bats on a String

Orange String Lights

Bubble Machines

Witches' Broomsticks

Monster Stickers

Paper Candy Corns

Apple Garland

Pumpkin Jar Lights

Feathered Ravens

"Happy Halloween" Banners

Pumpkin Wreaths

Dimly Lit Lanterns

Fog Machines

Vampire Coffin

Witches' Feet Hanging under Doorways

White and Orange Candles

Halloween Doormat

Jar of Eyeballs

Scarecrows

Skeleton in Sunglasses

Bubbling Cauldrons

Hay Bales

Pumpkin Balloons

Giant Fuzzy Rats

Black Cat Paper Cut-Outs

Halloween Throw Pillows

Pumpkin-Shaped Candy Dish

Winner

What's the best costume?

Elsa

Dracula

Tinker Bell

Werewolf

Merlin

Dinosaur

Little Red Riding Hood

Baseball Player

Black Panther

Baby Shark

Miles Morales

Pirate

Ghostbuster

Pikachu

Cat

Wednesday Addams

Winner

Mermaid

Alien

Doctor

The Wicked Witch of the West

Wrestler

Robin Hood

Zombie

Toy Soldier

Cinderella

Bowser

Ms. Marvel

Optimus Prime

Rey Skywalker

Batman

Captain America

Goku

Pretend you're getting a familiar!
Which of these critters will it be?

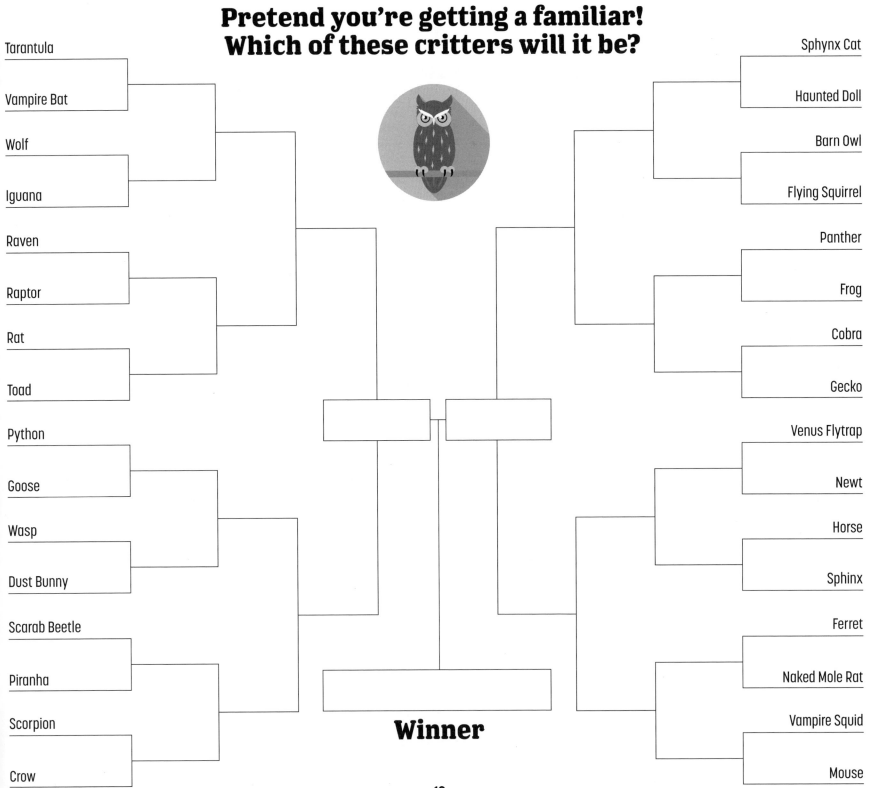

Tarantula

Vampire Bat

Wolf

Iguana

Raven

Raptor

Rat

Toad

Python

Goose

Wasp

Dust Bunny

Scarab Beetle

Piranha

Scorpion

Crow

Sphynx Cat

Haunted Doll

Barn Owl

Flying Squirrel

Panther

Frog

Cobra

Gecko

Venus Flytrap

Newt

Horse

Sphinx

Ferret

Naked Mole Rat

Vampire Squid

Mouse

Winner

What's the best candy or sweet?

English Toffee

Peanut Butter Cups

Chocolate-Covered Strawberries

Sour Lemon Drops

S'mores

Chocolate Chip Cookies

Caramel Apples

Rainbow Lollipops

Strawberry Mochi

Caramel Popcorn

Fruity Gummy Bears

White Chocolate Squares

Maple Doughnuts

Red Licorice

Candy Buttons

Candy Corn

Black Licorice

Cinnamon Rolls

Candy Canes

Chocolate Muffins

Jelly Beans

Chocolate Malt Balls

Marshmallow Rice Krispies Treats

Peppermints

Sweet Potato Pudding

Rock Candy

Gobstoppers

Cookies and Cream Fudge

Vanilla Ice Cream

Flan

Coffee Cake

Gingersnap Cookies

Winner

Which candy or sweet would you rather NEVER eat?
(Hint: It's like the last Bracketivity but in reverse!)

English Toffee

Peanut Butter Cups

Chocolate-Covered Strawberries

Sour Lemon Drops

S'mores

Chocolate Chip Cookies

Caramel Apples

Rainbow Lollipops

Strawberry Mochi

Caramel Popcorn

Fruity Gummy Bears

White Chocolate Squares

Maple Doughnuts

Red Licorice

Candy Buttons

Candy Corn

Black Licorice

Cinnamon Rolls

Candy Canes

Chocolate Muffins

Jelly Beans

Chocolate Malt Balls

Marshmallow Rice Krispies Treats

Peppermints

Sweet Potato Pudding

Rock Candy

Gobstoppers

Cookies and Cream Fudge

Vanilla Ice Cream

Flan

Coffee Cake

Gingersnap Cookies

Winner

You and your friends are going to wear a group costume! What's the best group costume idea?

Breakfast Foods

Disney Villains

Dinosaurs

The Addams Family

Astronauts and Aliens

Crayons

Toy Story Characters

Skeletons

Sports Players

Power Rangers

Teenage Mutant Ninja Turtles

Fairy Tale Characters

Star Wars Heroes

Rock Musicians

Disney Princesses

The Avengers

Sharks

Pokémon Trainers

Peter Pan and the Lost Boys

Transformers

Famous Painters

Stranger Things Characters

The Wizard of Oz Characters

The Justice League

Scooby-Doo and Mystery Inc.

Alice in Wonderland Characters

Safari Animals

Pirates

Ghostbusters

The Sanderson Sisters

The Incredibles

'90s Costumes

Winner

Which celebrity would you most want to star in the next blockbuster spooky movie?

Finn Wolfhard

Simu Liu

Jenna Ortega

Hailee Steinfeld

Millie Bobby Brown

JoJo Siwa

Tom Holland

Pedro Pascal

Awkwafina

Dwayne "The Rock" Johnson

Ryan Reynolds

Keke Palmer

Olivia Rodrigo

Dove Cameron

That Girl Lay Lay

Gaten Matarazzo

Taylor Swift

Charli D'Amelio

MrBeast

Harry Styles

Billie Eilish

Noah Schnapp

Selena Gomez

Pete Davidson

John Boyega

Zoe Saldaña

Iman Vellani

Sadie Sink

Dua Lipa

Zendaya

Halle Bailey

Florence Pugh

Winner

Imagine you meet a friendly ghost, but it's a secret. Where would be the best (or funniest) place to hide it?

Under Your Bed

In the Bathtub

In Your Closet

In Your Backpack

In a Garden

In Plain Sight

In the Basement

Under a Staircase

In the Garage

In the Dirty Laundry

In Your School Principal's Office

Under Your Desk

In the Couch Cushions

In Your Friend's Room

In the Toilet

In a Musical Instrument

In a Shoebox

In the Microwave

In the Pantry

In a Pair of Roller Blades

In a Fancy Purse

In the Car

In a Makeup Bag

In a Dog House

In a Towel Rack

In a Pile of Blankets

In the Pages of an Old Book

In a Trophy

In a Bowl of Fruit

In a Mug

In Your School Gym

In a Video Game

Winner

Imagine you and a team are putting on a haunted house and party. What's the best role?

Scare Actor

Costume Designer

Makeup Artist

Day-of Coordinator

Guest Greeter

Table Decorator

Set Painter

Lighting Technician

Manicurist

DJ

Snack Coordinator

Fog Machine Operator

Invitation Designer

Video Recorder

Special Effects Artist

Stunt Performer

Dessert Baker

Wardrobe Stylist

Tarot Reader

Poster Designer

Karaoke Manager

Clean-Up Crew Member

Prop Maker

Just a Guest

Pumpkin Decorator

Haunted House Tester

Candy Eater

Food Runner

Animal Trainer and Handler

Marketing Coordinator

Performing Musician

Fundraising Lead

Winner

Oh no! You *were* going to carve a pumpkin, but the pumpkin patch is empty! What are you carving instead?

Watermelon

Apple

Pineapple

Potato

Ice Sculpture

Honeydew

Cantaloupe

Plum

Bell Pepper

Orange Peel

Driftwood

Onion

Beet

Radish

Avocado

Tomato

Turnip

Stone Tablet

Eggplant

Banana Stalk

Cabbage

Coconut

Kiwi

Bread

Mango

Butternut Squash

Yam

Pear

Nectarine

Carrot

Strawberry

Dragonfruit

Winner

You're taking a celebrity to a haunted house. Who do you hope it is?

Chloe Kim

Kamala Harris

LeBron James

Serena Williams

Ryan Reynolds

Dwayne "The Rock" Johnson

Patrick Mahomes II

Harry Styles

Sasha Banks

Lady Gaga

Steven Spielberg

Billie Eilish

Samuel L. Jackson

Cristiano Ronaldo

Taylor Swift

Olivia Rodrigo

Ariana Grande

Shawn Mendes

John Cena

Vin Diesel

Tom Holland

Lupita Nyong'o

Tom Cruise

Rihanna

Liam Hemsworth

Henry Cavill

Venus Williams

Lionel Messi

Addison Rae

Simone Biles

Malala Yousafzai

Lizzo

Winner

Which character do you think would be the most fun to go trick-or-treating with?

Spider-Man

Garfield

Wanda Maximoff
(The Scarlet Witch)

Buzz Lightyear

Thor

Snoopy

Nick Fury

Mulan

Sonic the Hedgehog

Enola Holmes

Aang

Will Byers

Ash Ketchum

Cinderella

Mickey Mouse

Raya

Wednesday Addams

Mirabel Madrigal

Lucas Sinclair

Misty (*Pokémon*)

Robin (DC Comics)

Indiana Jones

Wonder Woman

Black Panther

Loki

SpongeBob
SquarePants

Obi-Wan Kenobi

Mavis Dracula

Meilin "Mei" Lee

Goku

Shuri

Draculaura

Winner

You've found a secret treasure room in a haunted house! Which treasure is the creepiest?

Baby Dolls

An Unfinished Map

Ship in a Bottle

Ancient Coins

A Golden Birdcage

A Destroyed Clarinet

An Engagement Ring

A Taxidermied Lion

A Jar of Worms

A Moth-Eaten Dress

A Broken Comb

A Marionette Puppet

A Gothic Mirror

A Preserved Hawk Skeleton

A Masquerade Mask

Torn Gloves

An Owl Statue

A Locket with Old Portraits

A Mummified Cat

A Melted Candle

Broken Glasses

An Old Pocket Watch

A Board of Pinned Insects

A Chipped Tea Set

A Portrait of a Clown

A Waterlogged Diary

A Jar of Eyeballs

Rusted Silverware

A Crystal Ball

An Embroidered Handkerchief

A Bracelet with Old Initials

Big Dusty Shoes

Winner

Your Halloween playlist contains all of the songs below. Which song is the best?

"Monster Mash" (Bobby "Boris" Pickett and The Crypt-Kickers)

"I Put a Spell on You" (Screamin' Jay Hawkins)

"Thriller" (Michael Jackson)

"Ghostbusters" (Ray Parker Jr.)

"This Is Halloween" (Danny Elfman)

"The Addams Family" (Vic Mizzy)

"I Want Candy" (Bow Wow Wow)

"Bloody Mary" (Lady Gaga)

"Time Warp" (Little Nell, Patricia Quinn, and Richard O'Brien)

"Highway to Hell" (AC/DC)

"Somebody's Watching Me" (Rockwell)

"Halloween" (Misfits)

"Ding-Dong! The Witch Is Dead" (Ella Fitzgerald)

"Look What You Made Me Do" (Taylor Swift)

"bury a friend" (Billie Eilish)

"Under My Bed" (Recess Monkey)

"Spooky Scary Skeletons" (Andrew Gold)

"The Monster Hop" (Bert Convy)

"Them Bones" (Caspar Babypants, feat. Outtasite)

"The Purple People Eater" (Sheb Wooley)

"Costume Party" (The Pop Ups)

"Spellbound" (Siouxsie and the Banshees)

"Ghost in the Closet" (Wendy and DB)

"Halloween Sharks" (Pinkfong)

"Superstition" (Stevie Wonder)

"Little Shop of Horrors" (Howard Ashman)

"Magic Dance" (David Bowie)

"Bumps in the Night" (KB Whirly)

"We Only Come Out at Night" (Smashing Pumpkins)

"Grim Grinning Ghosts" (Buddy Baker and X Atencio)

"Little Ghost" (The White Stripes)

"Season of the Witch" (Donovan)

Winner

What's the best spooky book or story?

Coraline

The Witches

Goosebumps

Ghost Squad

Bracketivity Scares

Spirit Hunters

Sorceline

Love Sugar Magic

Lumberjanes

The Witch Boy

Scary Stories to Tell in the Dark

Witchlings

Five Nights at Freddy's: Fazbear Frights

Bunnicula

Creepy Carrots!

"The Lottery"

"Hansel and Gretel"

The Spiderwick Chronicles

The Graveyard Book

The Girl Who Drank the Moon

Diary of a Minecraft Zombie

The Night Before Halloween

How to Catch a Monster

The Junior Witch's Handbook

The Last Kids on Earth

The Okay Witch

Bone Soup

A Series of Unfortunate Events

"The Monkey's Paw"

Spooky Pookie

My Big Fat Zombie Goldfish

The Spooky Wheels on the Bus

Winner

Imagine that you are peering into a crystal ball!
What do you hope is in your future?

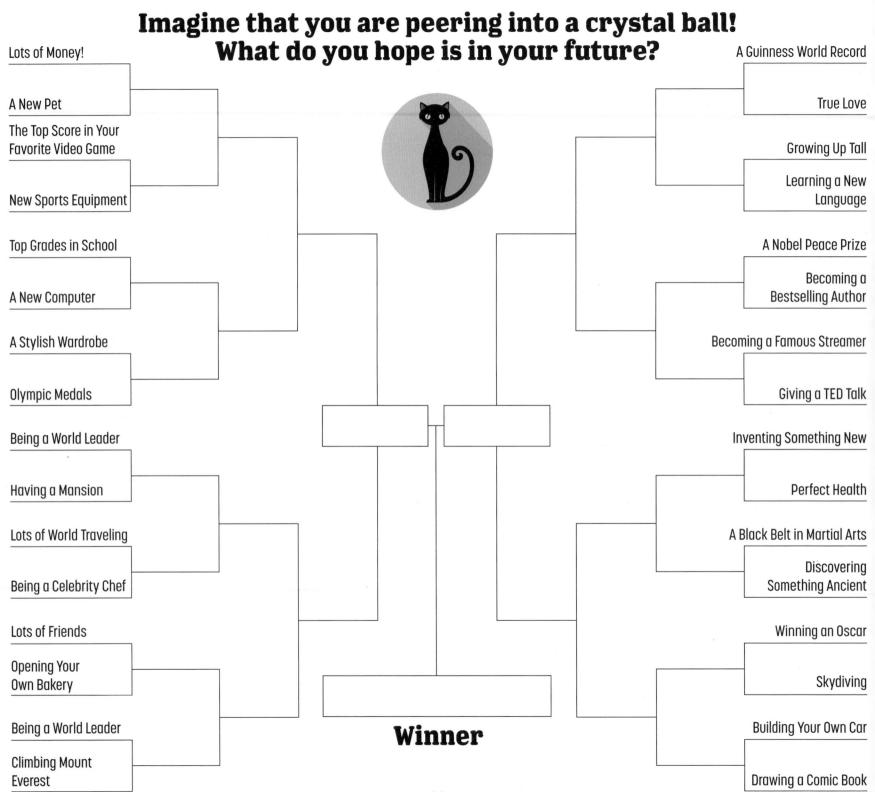

Lots of Money!

A New Pet

The Top Score in Your Favorite Video Game

New Sports Equipment

Top Grades in School

A New Computer

A Stylish Wardrobe

Olympic Medals

Being a World Leader

Having a Mansion

Lots of World Traveling

Being a Celebrity Chef

Lots of Friends

Opening Your Own Bakery

Being a World Leader

Climbing Mount Everest

A Guinness World Record

True Love

Growing Up Tall

Learning a New Language

A Nobel Peace Prize

Becoming a Bestselling Author

Becoming a Famous Streamer

Giving a TED Talk

Inventing Something New

Perfect Health

A Black Belt in Martial Arts

Discovering Something Ancient

Winning an Oscar

Skydiving

Building Your Own Car

Drawing a Comic Book

Winner

Which fictional villain would be the scariest to meet?

Kylo Ren

The Queen of Hearts

Count Dracula

The Wolf Man

Loki

Captain Hook

Thanos

Cruella De Vil

Ursula

Venom

William Afton

Lord Voldemort

Emperor Zurg

Sauron

The Joker

Mother Gothel

Darth Vader

Frieza

Emperor Belos

Lady Tremaine

The Evil Queen

The Wicked Witch of the West

Fire Lord Ozai

Bill Cipher

Plankton

Sid (*Toy Story*)

Bane

Mysterio

Maleficent

Team Rocket

The Spot

Harley Quinn

Winner

What's the best thing to drink on Halloween?

Candy Corn Milkshake

Cranberry Juice

Orange Soda

Hot Chocolate with Ghost-Shaped Marshmallows

Apple Cider

Strawberry Smoothie

Candy Apple Punch

Butterbeer

Frosted Lemonade

Pumpkin Pie Punch

Swamp Potion

Pomegranate Juice

Orange Sherbet Punch

Caramel Apple Smoothie

Grape Soda

Apple-Cherry Slushie

Apple Juice

Raspberry Lemonade

Bloody Shirley Temple

Mint Chocolate Chip Milkshake

Cherry Eyeball Punch

Banana Smoothie

Agua Fresca

Green Spider Smoothie

Pumpkin Spice Milkshake

Jack-o'-Lantern Float

Ginger Ale

Gummy Worm Punch

Vanilla Milkshake

Root Beer Float

Creamy Hawaiian Punch

Pumpkin-Apple Punch

Winner

What's the best chocolate to get on Halloween?

M&M's

Hershey's Kisses

100 Grand Bars

Reese's Peanut Butter Cups

Twix

Junior Mints

Milk Duds

Kit Kats

Rolos

Sno-Caps

Tootsie Rolls

York Peppermint Patties

Whoppers

Milk Chocolate Bars

Snickers

Andes Chocolate Mints

White Chocolate Bars

Milky Ways

Crunch Bars

3 Musketeers

Butterfingers

PayDays

Baby Ruths

Almond Joys

Hershey's Cookies 'n' Creme Bars

Heath Toffee Bars

Mounds

Toblerones

Dove Chocolates

Lindor Truffles

Mars Bars

Dark Chocolate Bars

Winner

Imagine you're carving a Jack-o'-Lantern. What kind of face or design are you giving it?

Toothy Grin

Angry Face

Skull and Crossbones

Mouse Ears

Cat Whiskers

Nothing!

Big Eyeballs

Surprised Face

Zombie

Heart Eyes

Witch Hat

Flowers

Candy Pattern

Frankenstein's Monster Face

Zombie Hand

Angel Wings

Scared Face

Puking

Anime Eyes

Tongue Out

Geometric Shapes

Zebra Stripes

Ghost Face

One Giant Eye

Fall Leaf Pattern

Kissy Face

Sad Face

Unicorn Horn

Silly Face

Cheshire Cat Grin

Polka Dots

Wizard Beard

Winner

Your friend is hosting a Halloween party! Which snack are you bringing?

Roasted Pumpkin Seeds

Veggie Burger Sliders

Pumpkin Spice Cookies

Stuffed Peppers

Sourdough Pretzels

Deviled Eggs

Sweet Potato Chips

Candied Pecans

Mini Pizza Bagels

Salt and Vinegar Chips

Mozzarella Sticks

Chocolate Chip Muffins

Apple Cider Doughnuts

Snickerdoodle Cookies

Spinach and Artichoke Dip

Pumpkin Hummus

Cheese Fondue

Potato Pierogies

Movie Theater Popcorn

Chips and Guacamole

Mini Quesadillas

Buffalo Chicken Wings

Mummy Hot Dogs

Veggie Chips

Jalapeño Poppers

Fried Mac-and-Cheese Balls

Sushi Rolls

Waffle Fries

Fruit Skewers

Cheesecake Bites

Sweet and Sour Meatballs

Halloween Puppy Chow

Winner

Write in your own:

With the following prompt, fill in your own Bracketivity!

Which of your friends would tell the best ghost story?

Winner

Many witches use a wand to cast spells. Of these, what do you think would be the coolest (or funniest!) object to use instead?

Math Notebook

Leaf

Cell Phone

Crystal Ball

Water Bottle

Watch

Feather Boa

Comic Book

Screwdriver

Hair Clip

Tarot Deck

Roll of Tape

Pencil

Smelly Sneaker

Pair of Knitting Needles

Volleyball

Microphone

Hair Comb

Quill

Colorful Candle

Paintbrush

Glue Stick

Ball of Yarn

Dog Leash

Bottle of Nail Polish

Sponge

Bookmark

Pair of Glasses

Laptop

Spoon

Old Book

Game Controller

Winner

Imagine you're helping a witch brew a potion. What would be the coolest potion to make?

Love Potion

Invisibility Potion

Cloning Potion

Hair Growth Potion

Shrinking Potion

Mind-Reading Potion

Immortality Potion

Friendship Potion

Shapeshifting Potion

Teleportation Potion

Sleeping Potion

Truth Potion

Lucky Potion

Laughing Potion

Healing Potion

Calming Potion

Animal Friendship Potion

Confusion Potion

Water-Breathing Potion

Energizing Potion

Memory Potion

Dancing Potion

Speedy Potion

Night Vision Potion

Super Strength Potion

Height Enhancer Potion

Just a Tasty Potion!

Fire-Breathing Potion

Disguise Potion

Quiet Potion

Artistic Potion

Inspiring Potion

Winner

Write in your own:

With the following prompt, fill in your own Bracketivity!

You get to decide what your best friend wears
for Halloween! Write in 32 ideas and
then see which one wins!

Winner

Imagine you're writing a horror story. Where would be the scariest setting?

Hospital

Summer Camp

Forest

Prison

Amusement Park

Abandoned House

Deserted Island

Desert

History Museum

Graveyard

Marina

Aquarium

Renaissance Fair

Water Park

City Hall

Football Stadium

Circus

Your Elementary School

Lighthouse

Zoo

Train Station

Community Pool

Vegetable Garden

Beach

Airport

Cave

Movie Theater

Shoe Store

Mall

Toy Store

Fire Department

Concert Venue

Winner

There are lots of scary monsters out there. Which of these monsters would you want to face the *least*?

The Demogorgon

Dragon

Frankenstein's Monster

The Headless Horseman

The Minotaur

Grendel

Cyclops

Dementor

Medusa

The Big Bad Wolf

Kraken

Cerberus

Mummy

Beetlejuice

Basilisk

Ghost

Vampire

Chupacabra

Banshee

Poltergeist

Mr. Hyde

The Wicked Witch of the West

Vecna

The Other Mother

Werewolf

Yeti

Giant

Sphinx

Hydra

Slenderman

Alien

Cthulhu

Winner

Werewolves are people who turn into wolves. (Fun fact: "Were-" means "man"!) Which creature do you think would be the coolest to turn into?

Cat

Horse

Fox

Ostrich

Tiger

Dolphin

Rattlesnake

Bee

Hummingbird

Elephant

Otter

Frog

Swan

Cheetah

Deer

Robin

Bull

Wolf

Peacock

Bear

Lion

Octopus

Mouse

Eagle

Platypus

Bat

Electric Eel

Giraffe

Rabbit

Penguin

Koala Bear

Meerkat

Winner

Write in your own:

With the following prompt, fill in your own Bracketivity!

What do you think would be the coolest name for a ghost? Come up with 32 ideas and then see which one's the best!

Winner

Of these, which do you think is the silliest costume?

Banana

Tyrannosaurus Rex

Whoopee Cushion

Pickle

Captain Underpants

Alien

Cow

'80s Workout Instructor

Snowman

Money Bag

Shrimp

Minecraft Zombie

Hot Dog

"Cereal" Killer

Baby Yoda

Taco

Rubber Chicken

Corn on the Cob

Sunflower

Waldo

SpongeBob SquarePants

Pencil

Pizza Slice

Wacky Inflatable Arm-Flailing Tube Man

Crayon

Fork

Hello Kitty

Skunk

Garfield

Clown

Scooby-Doo

Santa Claus

Winner

Write in your own:

With the following prompt, fill in your own Bracketivity!

Haunted houses can be scary alone! Who in your life would you most want with you?

Winner

Which of these creatures would you most like to trade places with for a night?

Werewolf

Ghost

Witch

Fairy

Changeling

Invisible Man

Ghost

Elf

Mummy

Dragon

Frankenstein's Monster

Ghoul

Slime Monster

Pixie

Goblin

Ogre

Vampire

Warlock

Shapeshifter

Mermaid

Satyr

Swamp Monster

Zombie

Yeti

Centaur

Werecat

Genie

Water Nymph

Robot

Banshee

Plant Monster

Leprechaun

Winner

Imagine you're following in Dr. Frankenstein's footsteps and making your own animal companion from scratch! Which feature will you include?

Sharp Claws

Big Eyes

Cute Toe Beans

Cat Tail

Deadly Fangs

Fluffy Fur

Forked Tongue

Feathered Wings

Pointed Ears

Horse's Body

Unicorn Horn

Rat Tail

Duck Beak

Eagle Eyes

Colorful Feathers

Long Whiskers

Rainbow Scales

Bat Wings

Floppy Ears

Long Snout

Button Nose

Long Tongue

Horse's Mane

Ostrich's Body

Invisible Body

Fish's Gills

Dog's Tail

Snake's Body

Owl's Face

Big Heart

Donkey Hooves

Bushy Eyebrows

Winner

Professions often make the best costumes! Which of these jobs sounds the coolest to dress up as?

Writer

Doctor

Gardener

Construction Worker

Cheerleader

Sailor

Farmer

Archaeologist

Chef

Scientist

Veterinarian

Judge

Astronaut

Horseback Rider

Yoga Teacher

Basketball Player

Painter

Preschool Teacher

Firefighter

Truck Driver

Lawyer

Race Car Driver

Nurse

Movie Director

Historian

Zookeeper

Sea Captain

Airplane Pilot

Rock and Roll Musician

Mail Carrier

Ballet Dancer

Influencer

Winner

Witches, warlocks, and wizards have incredible powers!
If you could have one of these powers,
which one would it be?

Healing Magic

Fire Magic

Psychic Magic

Summoning Magic

Reading Tarot Cards

Plant Magic

Telekinesis

Divination

Forcefields

Baking Magic

Weather Magic

Enchantments

Teleportation

Ice Magic

Illusion Magic

Music Magic

Potion Making

Animal Magic

Necromancy

Technology Magic

Water Magic

Shapeshifting

Protective Magic

Creation Magic

Hexes and Curses

Empathy Magic

Herbalism

Gravity Magic

Invisibility

Talking to Ghosts

Earth Magic

Reality Warping

Winner

Bugs can be spooky! Which bug or arachnid is the creepiest?

Worm

Scarab Beetle

Butterfly

Bee

Fire Ant

Termite

Tarantula

Millipede

Dragonfly

Grasshopper

Cockroach

Mosquito

Hornet

Weevil

Beetle

Praying Mantis

Caterpillar

Moth

Wasp

Cricket

Flea

Gnat

Firefly

Stick Bug

Louse

Leaf Insect

Daddy Longlegs

Scorpion

Mayfly

Damselfly

Fruit Fly

Stink Bug

Winner

Vampires often live in castles with secret lairs. If you had your pick, where would your secret lair be?

Old Castle, Duh!

Ancient Library

Science Lab

Indoor Pool

Crystal Cavern

Haunted House

Video Game Arcade

History Museum

Art Studio

Ancient Ruin Site

Skyscraper

Hospital

Animal Shelter

Water Park

Cruise Ship Cabin

On a Lake

Bookstore

Graveyard

Your School

Mansion

House with Legs

Art Museum

The Woods

Friend's Basement

Fashion Boutique

Your Favorite Restaurant

Ballroom

Local Bakery

Bathroom

Greenhouse

Zoo

Marina

Winner

You've just gotten a black cat familiar. Of these choices, what do you think is the best name?

Soot

Nightmare

Luna

Felix

Ash

Inky

Noir

Ziggy

Salem

Ophelia

Jiji

Halloween

Trick

Midnight

Winkie

Wednesday

Mittens

Void

Shadow

Cleo

Binx

Nero

Eve

Edgar

Onyx

Raven

Tigress

Athena

Thackery

Spirit

Licorice

Shadow

Winner

Some stories pit different creatures or monsters against each other. Of these choices, who do you think would win in a wrestling match?

Mummy

Ghost

Werewolf

Zombie

Boogeyman

Yeti

Dragon

Cyclops

Witch

Genie

Fairy

Three-Headed Serpent

Shapeshifter

Wizard

Kaiju

Phoenix

Vampire

Skeleton

Werecat

Unicorn

Kraken

Ghoul

Frankenstein's Monster

Loch Ness Monster

Pixie

Mermaid

Ogre

Chupacabra

Mothman

Gargoyle

Centaur

Banshee

Winner

Many water monsters live in a specific body of water. In which of these places would you most like to live?

Lake Tahoe

Mississippi River

Red Sea

Indian Ocean

Lake Huron

Amazon River

Missouri River

Caspian Sea

Niagara Falls

Dead Sea

English Channel

Arctic Ocean

Loch Ness

River Thames

San Francisco Bay

Panama Canal

Nile River

Gulf of Mexico

Lake Michigan

Mediterranean Sea

The Seine

Bay of Bengal

Sea of Japan

Chicago River

Atlantic Ocean

Pacific Ocean

Congo River

Suez Canal

Yangtze River

Yosemite Falls

Gulf of Alaska

Lake Superior

Winner

Imagine you get to make your own Halloween song. Which instrument are you sure to include?

Trumpet

Piano

Violin

Recorder

French Horn

Triangle

Drums

Banjo

Ukulele

Flute

Trombone

Xylophone

Bagpipes

Oboe

Harmonica

Tambourine

Cello

Electric Guitar

Harp

Clarinet

Bass

Mandolin

Tuba

Saxophone

Organ

Piccolo

Accordion

Bell

Marimba

Cymbals

Sitar

Vibraphone

Winner

There's a new spooky TV series on its way.
Where do you hope it's set?

Florida

Singapore

Romania

Czech Republic

New York

Iceland

Peru

New Zealand

India

England

France

Indonesia

Spain

Norway

Massachusetts

Brazil

Louisiana

Micronesia

Scotland

Korea

Ireland

Japan

South Africa

Oman

Colorado

Italy

Tanzania

Mexico

Argentina

California

China

Egypt

Winner

What is your favorite spooky video game?

Hello Neighbor

Hide and Shriek

Plants vs. Zombies

Survival Z

Black Book

The Legend of Zelda: Majora's Mask

Slender: The Eight Pages

Luigi's Mansion: Dark Moon

Costume Quest

Nancy Drew: Message in a Haunted Mansion

Five Nights at Freddy's

Cuphead

Hollow Knight

Bendy and the Dark Revival

Minecraft

Grounded

Five Nights at Freddy's: Security Breach

Psychonauts 2

Luigi's Mansion 3

Roblox

Costume Quest 2

Halloween Forever

Child of Light

Hotel Transylvania: Scary-Tale Adventures

Cozy Grove

Bendy and the Ink Machine

Five Nights at Freddy's 4

Hello Neighbor 2

Witch It

Fortnite

The Addams Family: Mansion Mayhem

Five Nights at Freddy's: Sister Location

Winner

Write in your own:

With the following prompt, fill in your own Bracketivity!

Who in your life do you think is most likely
to secretly be a vampire?

Winner

Now it's your turn!

Now that you're a pro at Bracketivities, you're ready to face any challenge!

Turn the page and make your own. You can also use this page to jot down any notes you have.

Winner

Winner

Winner

Winner

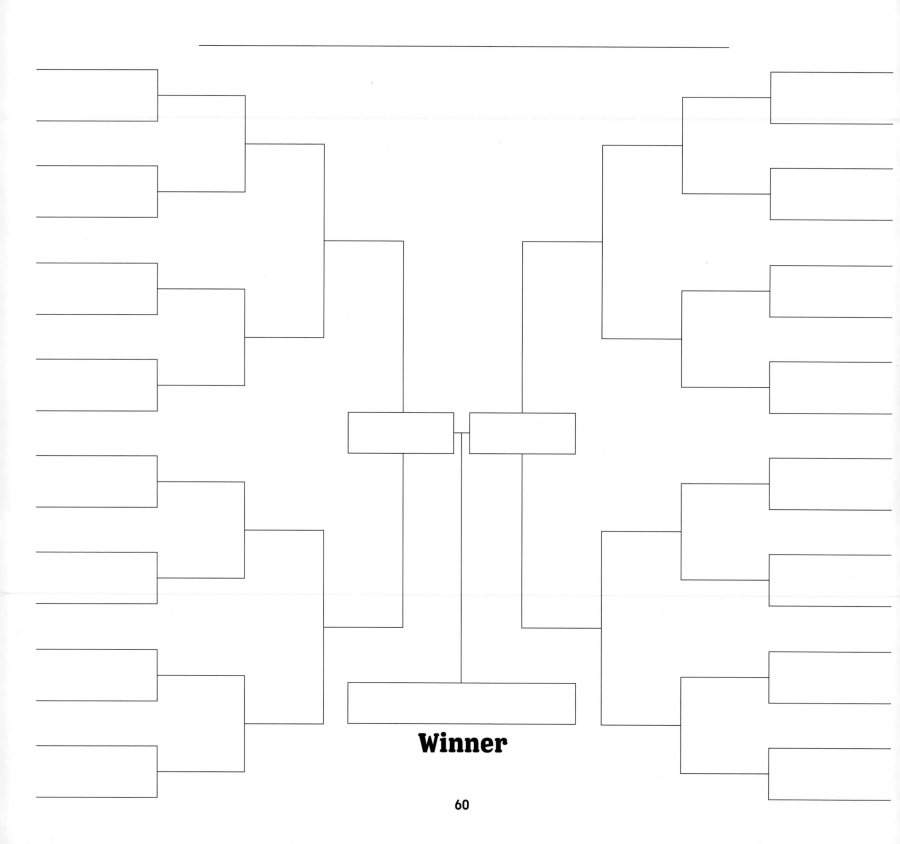

Winner

Winner

Winner

Winner

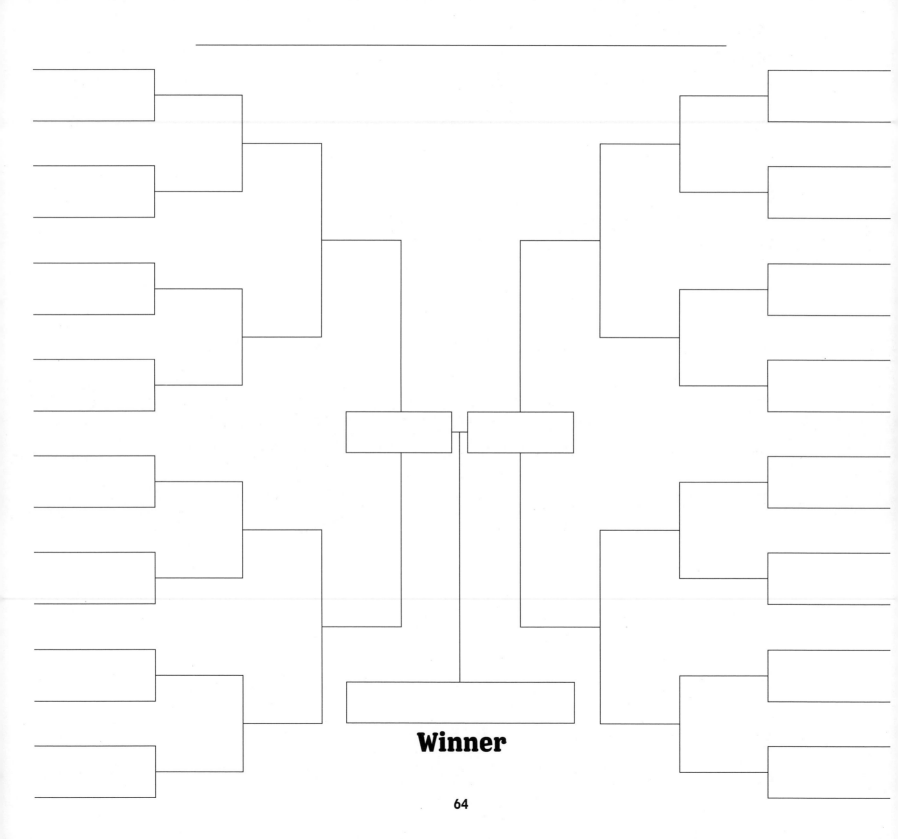

Winner